LOVE AT THE
EGYPTIAN THEATRE
Barbara Drake

Red Cedar Press
East Lansing 1978

Some of these poems have appeared in the following
periodicals: *Red Cedar Review, Three
Rivers Poetry Journal, Wormwood Review, Sumac,
Centennial Review, Michigan Hot Apples,
Northwest Review, Green Hous, Colorado
Quarterly, Marrow, The Lansing Star, Green
River Review, Hanging Loose, Centering.*

Cover by David Kirkpatrick

*Red Cedar Press/Review
English Department
Michigan State University
East Lansing, MI 48824
(517) 355-9656*

Preface

Look for her voice. It is an old-young voice, having both freshness and wisdom. The voice of a girl born in Kansas and, like Dorothy, destined to explore a more exotic world.

The voice is western, mid-western in its flatness through which a thread of melody, sweet observation, moves literally, relentlessly. The intellect is homely; it is swift and it is literal. I think it is American poetry, completely liberated from centuries of European culture and complete to speak autonomously.

I could be speaking about much of the New Poetry. No longer in thrall to English literature; no longer wanting to expatriate itself in European cities; no longer produced by a homogeneous education grounded in the classics. But I am speaking of Barbara Drake's deceptively simple, lovingly wise and sweetly melodic American poems.

She is a master of transforming the everyday (American) into a music that only those with the New Ears will be able to hear. She is strong and inventive and bold, and daring enough to write without excuses or sleight of hand. Once you have heard her voice it will haunt you. You will never go to a movie, a supermarket, your kitchen, or a bus station without hearing or wanting to hear her plain, insistent voice clarifying and focusing the American scene for you. She is already inside your secret love of paper, your erotic reaction to the plush seat at the cinema, and your inventive daily play with the language.

The first poem in the collection, "Imperfect Prisms," creates a paradigm of her poetic process which will intrigue and perhaps even obsess you when you discover it. She does know how to look at the world through many different lenses, and though she knows how the spectrum breaks down normally, she simply asks you, as you are seeing the light broken into a rainbow which possibly does not display

iii

this proper order, to look with excitement beyond that
order to how much beauty is there. Even in this plain, mun-
dane world, she makes her pure American declaration:

> I'd do it again.
> It was worth the price —
> getting seven
> apparently perfect rainbows
> from seven
> allegedly imperfect
> prisms.

Her poetry is one of acceptance and finally of rejoicing in
the act of acceptance as that act overcomes imperfection.
It is also the poetry of that great American dream — to do it
oneself. To make things. To make things better. To under-
stand them as a way of making them more complete. At the
end of "Talking To A Tree" she says,

> This morning,
> drinking my coffee in the tree-green light,
> I told it, "Okay tree, I get the message.
> Thirty-five myself and still —
> I've got to grow.
> Just give me room."

I do think if you let her voice into your head, it will pervade
you. I think that voice is clear and strong, melodically
simple and strange, and if you give it room, it will take up a
very big space.

Diane Wakoski
East Lansing
1978

For my family,
especially my parents,
Monica and Ward Robertson,
and my husband,
Albert Drake.

Contents

IMPERFECT PRISMS

They were having a sale
on imperfect prisms.
What's wrong with them? I asked,
Imperfect, said the salesman.

They looked fine to me.
I'm not perfect.
So I bought seven
and took them home in a box,
like hamsters
or a carton of fish,
and placed them in a row
on my east windowsill.
Then I went to bed in the dark.

Next morning
it was like when your dog
has puppies.
The white ceiling
wavered with young rainbows.

Prisms are pretty, you know,
but sharp. All
that morning, light
kept falling into the prisms,
breaking
and getting color
on my clothes and on my face.
I had my hands full.

I'd do it again.
It was worth the price —
getting seven
apparently perfect rainbows
from seven
allegedly imperfect
prisms.

1

GARBAGE

Watch out for the ones who insist
everything counts for something
and won't throw anything away.
They will bring you their used objects
which are never new cars or extra refrigerators
but are always stained baby clothes
or pickies that were canned by dead relatives.

They make clorox bottles into bird feeders
and popsicle sticks into Christmas decorations.
What optimists.
There will never be
that many birds or Christmases.

Still, it's their business
if their garages glisten with mayonnaise jars
or their highest cupboards harbor
unworthy bits of last year's cereal.
It's just when they want
to unload things on me
that I must speak up about garbage:
garbage, like guilt, is real.

I've got my own cupboard full
of old wool coats for a rug someday.
I've got a t.v. set
with voices and no pictures,
but *I admit,* it doesn't add up.
And I accept
that my best old wine bottles,
amber or green or clear,
may never again be anything but empty.
Even the two sides of one face
don't match exactly
because this material world
is much more complicated
than some people
would have you believe.

2

So let them keep their old children's board games
with several essential pieces missing.
If suffering brings them grace
or someone offers to buy
their twenty acres of used automobile tires
for a million dollars,
I'll offer my congratulations
but I won't, I won't, I won't
go looking
for old tires
or empty mayonnaise jars
or suffering.

THE MOUSE

I went to the kitchen early
one cool, spring morning,
past all of the others sleeping,
and warm in the tent
of my long flannel gown.
Bare feet on cold floors
remembered other morning floors.

The dim light came
like a breeze, sideways
through plants on the windowsill:
through orange and tangerine leaves
and the blunt avocado, through
spiney rosemary, and the fuschias
sprouted from four inch slips
carried halfway across the country.
It was a kind of kitchen forest
where I reached for the kettle
to brew my morning coffee.

And then I saw the cat,
the tortoiseshell mother cat
crouched staring into a crevice
between cupboard and stove.
Kneeling, I looked my way
into the dark crevice
and saw a mouse
transfixed by the cat's stare.

To study the mouse, the situation,
I placed my hands on the cat
and could feel her purr rise
with pleasure in this mouse.

It was a small mouse,
darker than the dust mice
I sweep from under the beds,

4

the white diaper of its underbelly
showing at the edges
of its blue grey pelt.
Its ears were soft and veined
as petals on spring violets.
Its boney feet were pink and
its whiskers were like
the bristles on a good brush.
I could imagine the string of its tail
dressed lightly across the knuckles of my hand,
if I were to catch it and teach it
to sit in my cupped palm
as I fed it small, parched corn
or a sliver of grape.
And since I was mother here
there would be no mother
to tell me whether or not
I might keep it. It was
all up to me.

Then I felt a tremor in the cat
and knew the moment had come
when the mouse would run
for safety under the sink.
And I thought of glasses and silver,
and fresh bread on the shelves,
and I thought of a mouse nest in the wall
woven round with the down of my towels,
and I thought of:
mouse tracks in the sugar,
mouse tracks in the flour,
the ravenous eyes of the mouse.

And I let
the cat
go.

LECTURE ON THE HEART

Let's understand,
a heart is something like a pill.
You swallow it,
it beats away, a timed capsule
without which you're just a shell,
looks nothing like a valentine.
A valentine heart is probably something sexual
dressed up in daddy's clothes, a male
genital disguised for mailing;
upside down, a Victorian lady's ass
pinched at the waist, and so on.
Or maybe it's one of those
linguistic mistakes, in fact a hearth
which might in turn have been a sort of grate
the Anglo Saxons used for roasting a haunch of venison
on the first day birds returned in spring
which is supposedly, Saint Valentine's day.
It's important not to confuse the real
with the imaginary and superficial,
such as red paper sentiments bordered by
good white intentions with holes in them
(probably made of scraps). A real heart
is more like a bloody radish,
crisp and hot and edible,
a fist-like muscle in the warm body,
always slightly off center in people.
In fact, Saint Valentine himself
also had nothing to do
with hearts or love or birds;
a Christian martyr of the third century, St. Val
sits next to Saint Vitus in the dictionary.
Saint Vitus, that's my patron,
a funny old uncle who taught me how to dance,
lit fireworks in the ganglia after dark,
forbid me one whole year to play in the heart,
as if it were a dangerous city park.

The heart is more like a room, actually.
I walked inside the one
at the Oregon Museum of Science and Industry,
a heart big as the museum bathroom.
I peered down the left ventricle,
and I peered down the right ventricle,
an irrelevant clot with a camera on my neck,
till the children pulled me through
and we went on to the lungs,
the clean white lungs of plastic
and the brown ones of the man who died smoking —
poor tarry paper bags
like wasp nests in their glass case.
On the other hand, I remember
the smallest heart I've ever seen
was the one that my friend Billy cut
out of the swallow he'd shot;
he put it on a blue plate, along with the liver,
for his sick yellow cat.
The cat would not eat,
continued to puke and die.
That day his mother was making sour cream fudge
which she poured to cool on a slab
of black and white veined marble.
Little bird hearts
make repulsive candy,
and I'd rather make soup
of my old valentines, simmer them
till the cupids like onions are soft
and the small hearts float to the top and burst,
which is how you know when hearts are done.
They pop.

      No, that's a lie,
and I promised to tell it straight.
That hearts break is purely mythical.
They just get stopped
or go limp and soft
like old leaky hot water bottles.
Unlike the famous woman fashion designer

whose lover shaved her pubic hair
in the shape of a valentine heart,
we will remember what the heart really is.
The heart is not genital.
It is not a public bathroom.
It is not made of paper or fudge or bird feathers.
The heart is not a martyr or a rare disease.
The heart, the heart, the heart
is a muscle.

LISTEN, DOCTOR

Listen, doctor,
all my life
I've had this thing for paper.
Do you think it's serious?
My mouth begins to water
in printers' shops.
As a little girl
I wanted to have
more rainbow tablets than anybody.
We didn't have much money
so I used to stand
outside the windows of art stores
looking at those expensive blocks
of watercolor paper, the kind
you wet and lift with a razor.
To me, real class is still watercolor paper.

My husband complains
when we go on vacation
I pack half the bags with paper;
notebooks, sketchbooks. . .
but I won't get caught in the sticks
without a tablet.
You should see my origami.
The lime is especially choice, and the red.
I've had this stash of origami papers
for years in the back of my desk,
in case of another world war.

Of course I discriminate.
Napkins, tissue — these are so-so.
Gift wrap is cute but dull.
Copy paper's bitter, squeaks
when you touch it, a modern
hysterical kind of paper I don't care for.
Kraft paper sacks are comfortable.
I've got a closetful.

Newsprint, lined and unlined,
has tooth and takes a soft pencil.

Often, when going for something simple
like a magazine, or sandwich bags,
I find myself buying a ream
of 20 lb. bond I don't really need.
Those blank sheets in a good stiff box
turn me on. Doctor, I need to know,
am I normal?

THE ANCESTORS

In those days
we lived in a cave.
We scraped the walls
pursuing fleas.
Our monkey feet
pattered down halls
blue as arteries.
We lit fires
and learned burning.
We killed a lot,
sometimes each other.
We knew only that self
ends at the skin,
and continual hunger.
Our children
grew up and up
until they were out
of sight.
We never let
our neighbors in.
Now, covered with vines,
we breathe as little
as possible.
No one believes
we are still alive.

THE WOMAN GETS RESTLESS

The woman gets restless
as the supper on the stove
is nearing completion.
Her fork tests a potato,
breaks a bit of meat,
salts the green vegetable.
Before the set but unsurrounded table
she stands in an empty house
listening for the sound of a car.
Whoever you are,
if you come at this time
she will feed you.

OLD FOLK TALE

One night
as I lay by my husband and he
was asleep
I heard a voice cry,
Rapunzel, Rapunzel,
let down your golden hair.

I rose and went to the window
and there far below was a man
in a fancy dress suit
of crimson and jet velvet.

Now my own hair is short and black
so I threw him the end
of the bedspread (yellow chenille),
and hand over hand he climbed
until I could smell his breath
like creme de menthe
and hear the jingle of his spurs.

You're imagining this,
I told myself, so
just as his hand crept over the sill,
Rapunzel is dead,
I whispered. *Take me!*

But he dropped to his horse
like an old movie cowboy
and fled.

SHE DREAMS HERSELF TITANIC

She dreams herself titanic
like the boat
that could not sink
but did not float,
and in her ears
what he lusts for,
crystal chandeliers.

Again the jewelled
iceberg tears,
again the waters pour,
again the voice of ice,
I'll ride you
to the velvet floor.
She wakes at dawn,
nine hundred miles from shore,
submerged and calm.

EARTHQUAKES

My eleven year old daughter is practicing
her school report on earthquakes.
Recitation of high catastrophe
shakes the late Sunday
living room.

　　　She says
there are 100,000 earthquakes or more
every year, 10 major ones;
100 destructive shocks, 1,000 damaging
shocks, 10,000 strong shocks and
1,000,000 little shocks.
Still, she goes on,
a trace of smugness in her clear voice
at having finished
this disastrous report
with such long, even numbers
and stretching it all out
to the required number of pages.
There is not even a tremor in her saying
13 million people have been killed
in earthquakes during the last 4,000 years.
More than one-point-five-million people
have been killed in just ten earthquakes
in the last 1,000 years. In 1923
an earthquake destroyed fifty per cent of Tokyo.
In Fukui, Japan, in 1948, the ground
opened and swallowed a woman
up to her neck; a cow also
was swallowed up to its neck.
(This is her required specific example.)

Outside our window
that crooked shadow of the apple tree
seems a black crevice opening in the snowy yard.
Callous little daughter, patching
your school report together, three pages
are not enough. The earth has swallowed
more than that.

MAGIC CHILDREN

My children, you grow so,
you make me feel like a joke,
a tiny car a lot of clowns
climb out of.

How you multiply,
from none to three.
Your father and I must be
an old vaudeville act,
and life is quicker than the eye.

Rabbits, red and yellow scarves,
fountains of paper flowers
spring from you.
Doves disappear
in velvet curtains
of your hair.

Oh, my magic children —
you saw me in two,
are my bed of nails,
the burning coals I walk through,
proof against wounds.

Loves, how shall I tell you
what I feel?
Like fans of cards,
eternal and unreal,
we must all fold back
into our own illusions.

LOVE AT THE EGYPTIAN THEATRE

Your father drives you
to the Egyptian theatre
and leaves you in front of
the dog-man-cat
which sits with its hands
on its giant lap
protecting the girl
in the lighted glass.
She takes your money
and gives you paper.

The movie is good
with three cartoons
and it's almost the end
when Buddy, your brother,
has to go to the bathroom,
so you stay in your seat.
You forget about Buddy
at the beginning
of the second feature.
It's good too.

After a while,
eating your jujubes,
tonguing their clear, dark colors,
and rocking your butt
back and forth on the seat,
you wish you'd gone
to the bathroom
when Buddy did,
but you stay—
for the whole second feature.
Then you watch
the first one over.

When the movies stop
and the lights go on
in the Egyptian sconces

with serpents and birds
on the ochre walls,
the music marches you
up the ramp of the aisles.
You're the last one out.

Behind you
the seats fill up
with shadows.

It was light when you got here.
It's dark out now
and the glass is dark
and the girl is gone.
You hug the theatre,
leaning on the posters.
A car goes past.
It's sort of like your father's car
but it goes on by.
You wonder where Buddy went.
It starts to rain,
halfway snow that turns to rain.
Another car slows down
but it doesn't stop
and it doesn't look
like your father's car.
Then no cars come
and no one sees you
but the cat-man-dog,
the dog-man-cat.

And there is no love
at the Egyptian theatre.

MOSS'S DREAM
AND A LULLABY FOR A SEVEN YEAR OLD BOY

He said he dreamed there was a store.
When you went into the store you grew old,
and when you came out you became young again.

I asked him why this frightened him. He said,
he had gone into the store and it closed
before he got out.

              There, baby, there.
Come into bed between mother and daddy,
to the warm center like a beating heart.
You are seven years old
and it's almost dawn.

There's no such place,
no such store, there is no store.

Say: there's no such place.

READING GRUN'S TIMETABLES OF HISTORY

I like the simplicity of the early years.
In 791 A.D., for example, nothing happened
except that the Byzantine Emperor, Constantine,
put his cruel mother in prison.
That was the year before
the Vikings conquered Ireland.

You can see the obvious patterns.
No one will convince me it was an accident
that in the year 1000 (when Beowulf was written)
an Indian mathematician, Sridhara,
suddenly recognized the importance of zero,
and there was
"a widespread fear
of the end of the world
and the Last Judgment."
Up until that time
they hadn't had a real zero year.
Minus four, after all,
was the "probable birth of Christ."
The next fifty
were skipped over rather quickly.
People who lived and died in those years
saw the crucifixion,
heard "The first definite reference to diamonds,"
and (if they were Romans)
"learned the use of soap from the Gauls."
Soap, diamonds, and crucifixions.
You understand what I mean.

And in 900,
the year in which
"Farces make their first appearance,"
what then? Well,
"Castles become
the seats of the European nobility."

And I believe
there must be a definite connection
between the abandonment of the bow
as a weapon of war
by the English army in 1595
and the appearance of heels
on shoes, that same year.
In 1596, just before water closets were invented
"by Sir John Harrington, courtier and author,"
Sir Francis Drake died.
To have died just before
the invention of the toilet! Well,
perhaps it seems more significant
from our historical perspective
but leave it to a writer
to invent them.

But now you've got my point,
for personal and egotistical reasons
let's skip some, to the year 1939,
when I was born and my husband-to-be
was four years old.
Yeats had just died.
This gives me the empty feeling
of racing into a station
just as a train pulls out
carrying an eminent and beloved person
who will never again be seen alive.
The station smells of steam and hot metal,
of wet wool and babies' diapers.
Over the noise of the engine
faint voices are singing "Lili Marlene."
In a nearby theatre, other voices are singing,
"Somewhere over the rainbow."
Italy invades Albania.
Roosevelt demands assurances
from Hitler and Mussolini.
Steinbeck wins a Pulitzer for *Grapes of Wrath*.
Gone With The Wind takes the Academy Awards.
William O. Douglas is named to the Supreme Court.

It is partly a matter of detail,
partly a matter of seeing
in retrospect the patterns
that were already there
even before the event
that makes it at once so clear
and increasingly confusing.
I expect it to get more so
before the year 2000.

April 13, 1976

GOOD FRIENDS AND FIRST IMPRESSIONS

I got a sunburn on my ass today, you said,
and flipping your tennis skirt
like an east coast can-can girl
you gave the party a peek. It was red.

If I hadn't known you better I'd have thought,
uh uh, look out for that one.
But I don't think that way any more.

At another party, ten years ago at least,
when I met you the first time,
you reminded me of a Captain Easy lady.
Your legs were curvy
the way they looked in comic strips in 1940.
You looked energetic enough
to jump aboard a passing Chinese junk
or wave from the deck of an aircraft carrier
at Easy flying by.

But you'd a baby in the car, and we were all
too poor to be adventurers. *Women don't like me,*
you said. *Too much hair and lipstick.*
But I liked you a lot. I'd see you pass our house
with the plaid stamp buggy full of bags and the baby.
You'd walk reading a *Vogue* or *Cosmopolitan,* such
other-than-grad-school worldly stuff, with a pint of Ripple,
red or white, in a paper sack.
You'd take a sip, push the buggy a few steps
and read of Jackie, whom someone told you
you resembled. Giving the baby a slice
of Wonder bread white as an angel, you'd stop,
offer me a snort from the bottle.
You've always been one of my most generous
and unsanitary friends.

Well, that's how you looked to me then.
Also: behind the hedge in your yard painting
enormous self-portraits. I thought

you were trying to find your own face
when all the rest of us dealt in words.
Or you, pulling something from a wrinkled
Goodwill sack and saying in your New England voice
that sounded foreign on our West coast,
I found this lovely gown today.

In the hospital, after my daughter was born
and I lay like a tube of toothpaste someone
had squeezed flat, you came
bringing your odds and ends of lotions,
lipstick, perfume, the kimona of rose-colored silk
to bring me back to life.

And you laughing heartily, and you in tears,
and you seeing whatever you have seen of me,
and now after ten years and moving with husbands
and children and dogs and rooms full of furnishings
thousands of miles we are: here again, in the same town,
turning up at the same parties, knowing
too many of each other's secrets to ever talk
at parties about anything but these
true and untrue first impressions.

AMELIA

I am impressed by the story
of my mother-in-law's neighbor,
a lady named Amelia
who looks like a side of beef on wedgies.
Amelia has grey hair
and every other word she says is,
"goddammit."
Indoors and outdoors, she wears a mumu,
smokes Camels, carries a poodle.
On fine days, when windows are open,
you can hear Amelia cough
all over the neighborhood —
"goddammit this. . .goddammit that."
She's outlived two husbands.
Here's the part that gets me.
When she ran off with the second one,
Amelia's first husband
drank prussic acid.
The neighbors say
she must be some woman.

1963, NOVEMBER 22

If you were anywhere,
you remember where you were
on November 22, 1963,
and the moment you heard the news
and who you turned to
and what you did then.
We've seen the reruns on t.v. so many times
they've gotten to be like old home movies,
or *Sunset Boulevard,* which also starts with death.

My clothes wouldn't fit
so I didn't get dressed all week.
I had a fire from cedar you had cut.
The baby was aleep when you called.

You and I had just come back
from going on-the-road.
We didn't have television,
or even a radio, so after you called
you came home.
We drove to my uncle's
and watched.

Everybody went on the road in those days.
There were freighters leaving for Tangiers
practically every hour; they were so cheap,
it was like they were free.
All you had to do was put your thumb out,
get to the dock, and fall in.
Next thing you knew, you were
walking around the Vatican.
Nobody got busted for dope;
we only touched wine;
wherever we went, people invited us in
(except Monte Carlo)
and we got to Korfu before the casino.

Coming back was even easier.
Out of money, we docked,
found a taxi in New York
and drove it west
for a hot-shot named Manny;
besides playing horses,
Manny dealt taxis
to a guy in Oregon who repainted and sold them.
Not bad, to travel coast to coast in a taxi,
and our shoes falling apart.

Manny fixed us up
with license plates
made of brown corrugated cardboard.
This perplexed the cops
who woke us where we slept one night
on the taxi seats, parked in an Iowa cornfield.
"Ever been to Cuba?" they asked.
"Gosh, no," we said,
and showed them passports stamped in red,
NOT GOOD FOR CUBA.
I was pregnant
and we had our English straight,
so they let us go.

Being back —that
was more difficult.
No one wanted to hire
two English majors, fresh off the road,
and one of them pregnant.
We moved to the woods,
ate welfare surplus wheat,
did what work we could.

After the baby comes,
we thought,
maybe we can join
the Peace Corps.

But it was November
before they slit me like a trout
and hauled the first-born out.
You'd found a job by then,
and I was feeling tender
that first day alone with him.

So there I am.
In the center of a one room cabin
with a new baby in an old crib,
and I am listening
to every breath that baby is breathing,
and I am looking at my own life
as if it were a sock
I've just realized
I'm wearing inside out,
and I'm about to turn it.
There is no one around
who knows our new phone number but you.
The phone rings and there you are.
You are telling me what has just happened
2000 miles away in Dallas.
It is 1963, November 22.

GAMES

We stop before the display
of the ancient Aztec city
in the small university museum.
On the giant pyramid, two feet tall,
"A priest rips out the heart
of a living victim,"
while on the playing field to the right,
"Players throw a large iron ball
through a metal ring.
Rather like basketball.
Losing teams are sacrificed to the gods."

Behind the playing field,
a rack displays fifty-thousand skulls, the losers,
strung like the beads of an abacus.
Aqueducts, sign of an advanced technology,
stretch beyond the geometrically pleasing city.

My daughter says, "I wouldn't play."
My son says, "I'd run away
and go somewhere else."
We are nice normal people.
We identify
with the victims.

Past the stuffed passenger pigeon,
the Chinese vases and the displays on transportation
I imagine the nightmare heaviness of an iron ball
which must be heaved up, up
into a circle of metal
from which it will fall back again, toward you.

There is no safety in this world.

WHAT A RELIEF

What a relief.
I've got a fever — 101
like the highway
down the coast.
That means it's real.
All week I've wondered
where I'm going.
Now I know. To bed
with orange juice
and magazines
and a country music station.

God bless me.
I'm starting to sneeze.
All week it's been
premonitions of disaster.
I've stayed low, avoided
crazed looking shoppers
in supermarkets,
air travel, and water.
Now, when my nose
starts to run,
it's welcome as a shower
after a dry week
of clouds and thunder.

How wonderful.
My throat is really sore.
Listen to my voice. It's going.
All week I thought
I might be having a nervous breakdown.
I thought I might be getting
psychosomatic premature senility.
I thought it was my liver
or something the government
was putting in the water.
Congratulations.
It's a cold.

THE MAN WHO INVENTED ONE

He was
a strange man, with a wart perhaps
signifying darkness, an outcast
who felt a need to name
what there was between one old toad
sitting alone under a stone
in the forest, and one man,
himself. There was no limit
to what a man might do, once
he had begun it: one,
and one,
and one. . .

Now we will
our way to light through equation:
one million stars of which
no two are the same star, days and nights,
equal and yet
not equal.

One day, we hope,
it will also be clear, what
numbers have to do with multitudes,
multitudes with solitudes. Meanwhile
there is one moon, one lamp post, one
whistling bicyclist — there are one
dozen eggs, five fingers to
one hand, one beginning and one end
for most of us.

IDENTIFYING ANIMALS

Have you thought of what it means
to be an animal? It means
to be capable
of spontaneous movement
and rapid motor response to stimulation.
You can walk, run, jump or fly;
throw up,
or twiddle your cilia.

Even if you hunch into your fur
or your feathers or scales,
your skin or shell,
your chitinous exoskeleton
or your bright glaze of gelatin,
and pretend to be a rock or vegetable,
sooner or later
something is going to
get a reaction from you.

You'll inhale
the breath of the bestial
and sneeze,
reproduce by fission,
or yell,
"Get in your own lane you sonofabitch."
Then everyone will know
you're not a lily of the field
or a mineral, content to erode
and go into solution.
Act is what animals do,
you animate
animus,
animal.

BUS FARE

Today, when I was looking you up
in the phone book,
I saw the Greyhound number
and thought of when
the children were all babies
and I didn't have a car.
Sometimes on winter afternoons
when the babies were taking their naps,
I'd call the bus depot
and ask how much it cost
to get to different places
like Baltimore, or Atlanta, Ga.
It was $68.50 one way to San Francisco,
forty bucks more if you came right back.
I almost called today
to see if the price had changed.
It was good to know
you didn't have to be rich
to get somewhere.

PORTABLE SHERWOOD ANDERSON

At the end of the
bicentennial summer,
a lady was traveling east
in a car that had seen better days,
traveling from Oregon to Michigan
for reasons that will remain unknown to us.
She was sitting beside her husband
reading a certain book
to pass the time.

Now I might as well tell you
the specific indentity of that book
was *The Portable Sherwood Anderson*
and I was that lady traveling
as I have every summer for ten years
the road between Oregon and Michigan,
for reasons we will continue to ignore,
since what matters is the journey itself
and the road and the book and the season
and the sense of the country one gets
from two thousand four hundred miles worth
of look-alike interstate rest areas.

Wherever we stopped,
in Oregon or Wyoming or Iowa,
all along Interstate 80,
there'd be the same big brick bathroom
with the same electric
hot-air hand-dryers (for our protection)
and the same redwood information centers
and picnic benches and pet walking areas.
In Idaho or Illinois or Nebraska,
I'd ride along reading
The Portable Sherwood Anderson
and when I looked up, there it would be —
something brick that looked just like
the last one.

The Stuckeys and Texacos
were cut from one design
and Little America
was a great big gas station.
A sad feeling slipped over me
like the dark at the end of summer
on the eastern ends of time zones,
a sadness at how one place was getting to be
too much like another,
tasteless and conveniently speedy
like a factory hamburger.

And then it happened,
just this side of Laramie,
or Kearney—or Joliet,
as we pulled into a rest area
with a statue of Abraham Lincoln,
where a CB radio club
was passing out free coffee in styrofoam cups,
and giving away red, white and blue bicentennial
anti-litter bumper stickers,
which a guy in a blue Dodge pickup
with a "love it or leave it" sign took two of
and left,
as did the couple in the van
with airbrush gargoyles all over it
and a diffenbachia hanging in the rear window.

It happened so quickly,
I almost didn't notice the boy in embroidered levis
calling and calling on the payphone,
calling to someone who didn't answer.
He knocked his forehead against the payphone,
gently, gently, waiting
for someone who didn't answer.

And I almost didn't see
the family of eight climbing out of the station wagon
with charcoal and lawn chairs,

beach balls and steaks,
a parakeet in a green plastic cage
and battery television.

When I spotted the traveler,
I was so intent on reaching him,
I walked past the mini-bus named "Utopia,"
past the red-haired cowgirl
and the latin-looking man with five poodles;
I almost stumbled over the old couple
announcing the end of the world.
I took one of their pamphlets that warned
we would all be devoured pretty soon
by a beast that resembles Godzilla,
but I brushed them off politely
and made my way toward the stranger
with sad, familiar eyes.
I thought he might be a relative of mine
for he looked like a misplaced dreamer
or a failed chicken farmer
who had come to this rest area
like some kind of mid-American
ancient mariner.
I thought he was eating his lunch
for he had an egg in his hand
but he didn't crack it or eat it.
He just looked at it, turning it around.
He stared at the egg.
Then he looked at me.
I looked at him.
He looked at the egg again, reflectively.
And then I asked him.
Clutching my *Portable Sherwood Anderson,*
standing in an obscure rest area on Interstate 80
somewhere west of Rawlins, or Davenport, or Gary,
I stammered my question.
"Mister—don't I know you from somewhere?
You famous or something?"

"Could be," he answered.
"No one knows more about eggs than I do."

LONG DISTANCE

Judy called tonight to say
her phone bill last month was $187,
a new record for her.
It worries her, as if
the phone bill were a thermometer
that says she's sick.
That's why she called.
"It must mean I'm sick.
Do you think so?"
I hope to say the right thing.
I tell her, "No."

I wonder if it really frightens her
or if there's some comfort
in the affirmation of that bill
that she does feel really rotten,
as when you think it's in your head until
you find your fever is 103.
To have a friend who has been
calling long distance at night
for years is a heavy responsibility.
What can I say that would be worth it?
"Probably cheaper than a psychiatrist,"
is good for a while, but now
it may be time for a new look
at the situation.

How about a Marxist interpretation?
Judy, this bill is unfair.
Long distance should cost no more
than a call to the local drugstore.
You've got a job in Iowa.
I've got a job in Michigan.
The man you love works in Montana.
Your mother's in Oregon.
Your cousin's in Pennsylvania.
Your daughter is visiting

your ex-husband in California.
And so on.
If these were the old days,
we'd probably all live within
a mile of one another
or not know each other at all.
The telephone is not a mere tool
of communication, it's a time warp
through the zones,
a relative leap through space,
a necessity in this populous but lonely
neighborhood McLuhan called our "global village."

Judy, you may be out of money,
and you may be lonesome
but you're not sick,
it's the system.

TRAVELERS

I'd been trying to take up room on the bus
so no one would sit with me.
I read my Trollope novel ostentatiously
as I ate chocolate covered toffee.
In my purse I had a peach
with skin like the finest flannel
and the color of a full moon
when it first comes up in October.
I was saving that for later.

Then a boy of the road got on;
how can I express
his joyless meagerness?
His pants hung on his butt
like an old paper sack.
He had a frayed khaki pack.
Of course, he sat by me.
Taking out his cardboard covered journal, he wrote,
"Monday. Fog on the coast."
That duty performed,
he studied his map and ticket,
good all the way to Eureka.

Feeling guilty,
I almost started a conversation
as ladies sometimes do on buses
to younger persons, but he gave me
such a look of disapproval.
When he took out his bag of granola and prunes
I could not get back to my Trollope and chocolate
fast enough.
        The dried oats stuck to his lips.
I wish I had not let him sit there.
The peach stayed in my purse.

HERE WE ARE

in sunny California
at the Lodi Rod Run. A June day,
it's 104° and I hate it.
The children and I flop around like
old grease rags on the car seat,
the car our only shade.
We do this, look at hot rods,
for your sake, husband,
but not too cheerfully.
What do you expect?
Love me, love my fantasies?
Forget it. Love you is enough
in this metallic heat.

Nearby, a crowd of hot rodders,
men and their hot rod wives,
discuss this year's Lodi Rod Run T-shirts
and how the women's are not big enough
in the bust. The women berate their men
more offensively than I would,
each saying rather proudly,
"You expect *me* to get into *that*?"

Forget about Lodi. Now
I'm on the track of a scene
from my own past.
Father is leaning on the fence
talking to the man in leather
by the air strip.
Mother and I sit
in the old black Buick.
I'm playing I can drive it.
We've been sitting there at least an hour.
This is our regular Sunday drive.
I flop the steering wheel
and try to reach the pedals.
I want to get going.

Mother says,
"Watching people can be quite fascinating.
Look at that man and woman.
I think they're fighting."
The woman has hair
the color of a cherry coke.
She's a woman who walks
with her coat bundled to her like a bathrobe.
Cigarette in one slim hand, she is graceful,
tense, growing old quickly.
We can't hear through the glass
but sure enough, abruptly she turns from him.
He makes a movement of conciliation
which she doesn't see, then goes
in the opposite direction.

A family files out of the airport cafe.
"They must be related," says mother.
"They all look like potatoes."
We turn on the radio and laugh
at how they start walking to music,
potato, potato, potato.
(An illusion, I know, a trick,
but it works so well
sometimes I still do it.)
Out by the fence
father's mouth forms words like
"DeHaviland Dove" and "Handley Page Harrow."
Mother finds a stick of gum in her purse.
We divide it.
We roll down the windows
to let a breeze in,
but the orange windsock is limp.
Grasshoppers click
in the tan grass off the air strip.

Back to Lodi.
Now you have a new pal.
Who he is, I don't know,
but both of you are saying almost in unison,

41

"Bonneville in '56," and "manifold."
You are saying, "Road Angels" and "headers,"
"modified '32 engine" and
"Southern California Timing Association."

The children fuss.
I rummage around and split
the last stale donut.
There's warm Kool-Aid in the thermos,
and in my purse,
enough lifesavers to go around,
once.

Husband, framed in the car window,
machine love animates you
even at high temperatures,
but why am I here?
Old songs on the car radio
make it appear
I move to music
even I can't hear.

TALKING WITH A TREE

What are you?
Some sort of laurel — an avocado?
I don't know.
A stem and three flat leaves, a ten
year old tree with just three leaves
in a rusty can decorated once by Suzy
my sister when she was a brownie.
(She's a sophomore in college this year.)
What do you live on tree?
You've no dirt left.
You must be eating your own can.

Listen.
I don't go in for cruelty to trees.
I've just been busy these past ten years,
three kids, one thing and another.
But I did notice you, how each time
you tried for that fourth leaf
one of the others fell off. I thought
you'd only got three leaves in you.

Your tiny trunk looks like a fakir's rope,
tough, standing straight up,
supporting those three leaves like magic.
When we moved, you toppled in the U-Haul,
looked pretty dead, I thought.
With water you pulled through.

That summer we went away, I took you
out in the back yard.
Humming "Born Free"
I set you out. I said,
"Make it on your own, plant."
In September, I returned
to find you at my door,
wasted, thin, and brown.
With water, you came back.

43

Tree, modest three-leaved tree
growing without dirt or attention,
what do you want from me? Okay.
I'm going to get you out of that can,
into something befitting your experience,
a big clay pot with lots of acid soil in it,
stones at the bottom for drainage and
all that garden book stuff. You're tough.
It's time I did right by you.

So, I did it. And on the second day
the tree arose from the living dead,
put on six leaves, then nine, twelve,
fifteen and eighteen. The leaves were all
different shapes for a while,
coming on like valentines,
leaves like green bats, green birds,
I-love-you-I-love-you leaves,
green banana leaves,
some plump as the faces of babies,
one broad and magnanimous as a sun hat.
It had a leafing-out orgy.
It gave itself a regular birthday party.

I almost didn't like it.
It wouldn't fit in the window anymore.
But I gave it a sunny spot on the kichen floor
and let it rise.

          This morning,
drinking my coffee in the tree-green light,
I told it, "Okay tree, I get the message.
All these years myself and still —
I've got to grow.
Just give me room."

FIELD POEMS

1

Downtown in my car
coming to a parking lot
getting out on the hot
blacktop: a bunch
of blue chicory
was coming to bloom
in a space of dirt
about the size
of a brick
and some milkweed
came up at the edge
where the building
and blacktop
hadn't quite stuck
together. As if
I'd found a hand
coming out of the
sidewalk, I cried
in surprise,
There's a field
buried under
this city.

2

In the golden houses
of summer grass,
the tent houses
of tall straw grass
tied at the top
with more golden grass
and some green
and hollowed
by backing in slowly
bottoms rounding a space
in the still rooted
sheaf of grass,
we lived for a summer
on the wild blackberries,
the small and large kinds,
and made another house
under the bramble patch
of berry vines
and another house
in the morning glory
and houses we didn't even
stop to live in, just forgot
as soon as we'd finished them,
and houses so perfect
there have been no such houses
since in my life, and ate
apples and three kinds of plums
from the old trees,
were self-sufficient,
and sometimes ate clover
which grew at the edge
of the field and the woods
where we seldom went
because it was dark
and an old woman
was said to have died there
alone. And we were
too young to die,
ever.

3

There's a business going in next door.
First thing they chopped down
was the flowering plum tree.
It had been planted
by the old couple that lived there
when it was a farm and a field
right up to a year ago, planted
when they were a young couple.
When I asked him why he was chopping,
the man stopped his axe, laughed at me,
said, *A place of business*
does not need trees.

When the old people were still there
and complained about the rising taxes,
the township engineer said,
Be reasonable. After all,
this property is too valuable
to live on.

4

One year, that corner
was nothing but a marsh,
nothing there but cattails,
water, willows, coons and
possums, pheasants, foxes,
red and black birds.
Next year, there was blacktop,
cement, a shopping center
with sixty-seven stores.
Shortly after it opened
a man went mad there,
drove his car around the
blacktop at high speed,
making wider and wider
circles, people jumping
out of his way like frogs
on a rainy road,
running for the safety
of the shopping center.
Just before the police came,
he made a final spin
and disappeared.

5

How to plant a wild hedge:
string a wire across an empty field.
In a few years there will be a hedge
of wild honeysuckle, wild grape, asparagus,
or any other berry-seeding plants eaten
by the birds who will sit on your wire.

6

What's in the empty field
behind my house?
Dandelions, butter-and-eggs,
penstemens, hawkweed (red,
yellow, and orange),
chicory, nightshade, milkweed,
cinquefoil, daisy, fleabane,
wild purple asters, white asters,
goldenrod, sumac, wild grape,
yarrow, queen anne's lace,
gobo (burdock), sticktights,
winter cress, mustard, thistle,
poison ivy, wild rose, asparagus,
wild strawberry, moss, lichen,
many different kinds of grass,
wild honeysuckle, mullein,
red clover, white clover, sweet
purple clover;
foxes, pheasants, possums, racoons,
rabbits, orioles, finches, grackles,
doves, hawks, sparrows, blue jays,
to begin with.
For sale signs,
will-build-to-suit signs,
zoned commercial signs,
earth movers, dump trucks,
asphalt, concrete, brick and
glass and steel
to end with.

ROSES ARE HEAVY FEEDERS

Roses are heavy feeders,
ravenous as cats when deprived;
I feed them dried blood,
dust of bone to keep them
satisfied, and still
you've seen them scratch.
Now here is Garnet, the baby,
and Katherine T. Marshall,
Angel Face, Peace, Forty-niner,
to name a few. The ramblers
are off by themselves
all over the fence.
Roses must be free.
When you get them
tight in a bag or a pot
you'll find their roots
snarling and spinning around.
Like us all, they need to get out.
Spread their roots.
Give them room.
Make them free and remember that
roses are heavy feeders.

IN THE END OF MARCH

Your mother calls you
in the end of March
to come and eat
your mother calls you
in the end of March
her voice sings through the dusk
the first long evening
and mud beneath your boots
in the driveway quivers.

Long white arms
long white arms
mother mother
long white arms
of snow here and there
embrace the ground
for one last time
in the end of March
your mother calls you
when the snow gods go, go
and you go
to the house
where your mother calling
her invisible voice
like long white arms
says come to supper
come to supper.

You enter the house
with cold-red cheeks
you enter the smells
of brown roast beef
you enter the house
of your mother calling
enter the voice
of your mother calling
you enter the mother

the smell of the dinner
you enter the smell
of soap of vinegar
you enter the smell
of wax of gravy
vinegar gravy soap and wax
gravy cold cream soap and vinegar
roast beef cabbage soap
old newspaper.

The house beneath your feet
in this long dusk quivers.
The end of March
the end of March.
Mother mother
let me in.

SHE HOPES THIS IS NOT THE BEGINNING

She hopes this is not the beginning
of something worse
than what she was once
in the narrow past.
Hopelessly dirty, she liked
the sound of rain outside
and inside a rain-like music.
Dirty-dishes — she lazily poked them
with a greasy knife to find
the can opener.

On Saturday mornings she slept
later than ever, a thirsty night
all part of a dream now,
and woke to spend the day
drinking coffee and reading
in a torn bathrobe
with an elegant velveteen collar
and in bare, dirty feet.

Supper was mainly a poem
or lovemaking on an unmade bed,
then a cigarette shared
and an evening of company
or a ride on the bike
to some place
where there would be people.

What possesses her now
to wash the dishes right after supper,
empty the ashtrays and spend
hours in the kitchen or choosing
the best soaps for the washing?
Is it good to wear nylons and go
to bed by eleven,
to rise and make pancakes
with syrup by seven?

It may not be kind,
or even fair
to ask these questions.

DREAMS ABOUT TEETH

are almost common as teeth:
your caps fall from your mouth
like squash blossoms from the plant;
teeth crumble on food
as if they were made of crackers,
or pop from the gums
bloodless and wet as watermelon seeds.
Your dream may warn you
a tooth is about to split
like a sidewalk thawing,
or you imagine teeth
which grow in the wrong places
as in the end of thumb and forefinger.

Treacherous teeth,
you refuse to last one lifetime
but like cowards bragging after a battle
identify us in death
by the pattern of our expensive fillings.

How young I was
and how young my mother was
when she first took me to the dentist
already imperfect
with my rotten little teeth
like kernels of bad corn. They hurt.
They hurt more than any
hot chloroform drops
or oil of clove could assuage.

How old the building was
and how old the dentist,
a novacaine-furred beast
with hands cold-creamed like a lady's.
His glasses reflected my fear.

Get me some water, I said.
There's a rock in my shoe.

There's something outside the window.
I need to look.

But he killed me with gas.
Oh, mother.

Then there was the dentist
who pulled two teeth
and sent me back on the street with a bill
before mother got the car parked.
And Dr. Baker—
until his tractor rolled over,
and Dr. Wu, Chinese, who was so good,
replacing Dr. Baker's fillings.
And allegorical Dr. Dark
who fixed the tooth I had broken
on gravel, eating lentils in Greece.
Then there was the endodontist
who did the root canal
on the tooth Dr. Dark had crowned,
and the extractionist who pulled the tooth
when the root canal failed,
and Dr. Luke who built the gold bridge
to gleam in the space left by that,
and who has been drilling
and capping and cleaning and filling
my teeth for ten years now.
(I've settled down.
I'm letting my teeth fall apart
in one town.)

Oh, teeth,
you do not bite right.
You make my jaw crack.
I grind you.
You have a yellow stain
from when I had the measles
at the age of four.
(So says Dr. Luke. How wise.
He reads my past in my teeth,

sordid story
of an imperfect life.)
Well, Queen Elizabeth the first
had dead black teeth
in a pock-marked face masked
with ground bones and egg-white.
Thank God for progress and modern technology.

The language of dentistry
is so much more appealing than the process.
A crown, a cap, a bridge, a canal — it reminds me
of something royal and medieval.
But they have these machines, these robots,
all graceful metal elbows and insect arms.
The little table is a pinched pie crust,
a waiter's tray, a platform in space.

You put your cup in its place
and water tumbles into it.
The ice blue glassware, the sterling silver
instruments.
A giant molar on the windowsill, with plants.
Colorful prints of peridontal disease,
muzak, and ceiling tiles
in which the pattern is mathematically
irregular.
The comforting technician
uses the first person plural
as she cups your chin in her plump, warm hands
and clucks like a concerned mother
if you do not floss right.
The fillings are plastic.
The drills are all high speed,
and though there is a sinister smell of heat,
the pain is minimal and over quickly.

Still, your hands sweat.
Still, you want a drink of water.
The rock in your shoe has gnawed to the bone
but there's nothing else to do.

The first cavity is the first Fall.
No wonder dreams of teeth are common.

HOW WAS IT?

You know something I like?
It's after a party
when the sun comes up —
if there are still
two or three friends left,
maybe somebody
wakes up on the floor
or gets their second wind
taking a run around the block.
You wave at the street cleaner
or take a piss in the alley,
and then
you start to talk.
Dumb friendly talk like,
did you see old so and so,
or *did you get a load of*
me when. . .

Dying could be like that.
It wouldn't be half so bad
if you could sit around and say,
did you see me when I got my
head lopped off?
Or, *how about that? Front page*
in three counties!
And me so dignified.
You'd all laugh
and think how you'd died.
Though you had to pay for it after
with a bad taste or red eyes,
you'd feel good
about each other,
and get on then
with something else.

But what I don't like is
being alone
with all those dirty plates

and the wet butts in the bottles.
The room smells like dirt
when you're alone there.
With nobody to talk to about
how it was.

KNOWLEDGE

I ask myself what I know
at thirty-eight and
two degrees past high school.
I know something about people,
something about poetry,
how to bake a quiche so it won't curdle,
how to swing a hammer for nailing cedar.
I've forgotten the constellations I knew once.
I'll learn them back!
These answers are somehow unsatisfying.

Whatever I know
only touches the surface of things
as water spiders do,
thought riding the silvery film
of pressure meeting pressure.
I do know
it's not tension alone
that keeps water spiders afloat.
I saw in a book
how each holds tiny balls of air
clenched in its insect fists.
Fist?
That claw, hand, nail, or—pincer.
What do you call the digit of an insect
by which it holds a pearl of air
and thus contrives to walk on water?

A thing worth knowing
which I don't.
We should live forever.

Printed March 1978 in East Lansing
for the Red Cedar Press by Michigan State University Printing.
Text is set in 11 pt. Optima.
The Red Cedar Press also publishes the
Red Cedar Review, a bi-annual magazine
of the arts.

Photo: Harry Smallenburg

Barbara Drake was born in Abilene, Kansas, in 1939, but grew up in
Oregon. After attending the University of Oregon, as a graduate
and undergraduate, she moved to Michigan with her husband and
children in 1966. She is currently teaching in the Department of
American Thought and Language at Michigan State University.
During the summers she lives on the southern Oregon coast.